# CALVARY AND THE MASS

*Two Summits of Grace*

## FULTON J. SHEEN

Bishop Sheen Today
280 John Street
Midland, Ontario, Canada, L4R 2J5
www.bishopsheentoday.com

Library of Congress Cataloging-in-Publication Data

Names: Sheen, Fulton J. (Fulton John), 1895-1979, author. | Smith, Allan J., editor.

Sheen, Fulton J. (Fulton John), 1895-1979. Calvary and the Mass: A Missal Companion. Registered in the name of P.J. Kenedy & Sons under Library of Congress catalog card number: A 93597, following publication April 1, 1936.

Smith, Al (Allan J.) editor – Lord Teach us to Pray: A Fulton Sheen Anthology. Manchester, New Hampshire: Sophia Institute Press, 2019, ISBN 9781644130834.

Title: Calvary and the Mass: Two Summits of Grace.

Fulton J. Sheen; compiled by Allan J. Smith.

Description: Midland, Ontario: Bishop Sheen Today, 2021

Includes bibliographical references.

Identifiers: ISBN: 978-1-990427-48-0 (paperback)

ISBN: 978-1-990427-49-7 (eBook)

ISBN: 978-1-990427-14-5 (hardcover)

Subjects: Jesus Christ — Seven Last Words — Calvary and the Mass — The Eucharist

DEDICATED TO

*The Immaculate Mother of God*

WHO MOTHERED CHRIST
AS BOTH PRIEST AND VICTIM
AND WHO MOTHERS ALL PRIESTS
BOTH OFFERERS AND OFFERED
WITH HER DIVINE SON.

MAY SHE MAY,
THROUGH THESE PAGES
WHISPER TO US AS AT CANA
"WHATSOEVER HE SHALL SAY
TO YOU, DO YE"

*Ad maiorem Dei gloriam
inque hominum salutem*

*Jesus calls all His children to the pulpit of the Cross, and every word He says to them is set down for the purpose of an eternal publication and undying consolation.*

*There was never a preacher like the dying Christ.*

*There was never a congregation like that which gathered about the pulpit of the Cross.*

*And there was never a sermon like the Seven Last Words.*

**Archbishop Fulton J. Sheen**

# THE SEVEN LAST WORDS OF CHRIST

### The First Word
*"Father, Forgive Them
For They Know Not What They Do."*

### The Second Word
*"This Day Thou Shalt Be With Me In Paradise."*

### The Third Word
*"Woman, Behold Thy Son;*

*Behold Thy Mother."*

### The Fourth Word
*"My God!  My God!
Why Hast Thou Forsaken Me?"*

### The Fifth Word
*"I Thirst."*

### The Sixth Word
*"It Is Finished."*

### The Seventh Word
*"Father, Into Thy Hands*

*I Commend My Spirit."*

# CONTENTS

# PREFACE

*And it came to pass, that as He was in a certain place praying. When He ceased, one of His disciples said to Him Lord, teach us to pray, as John also taught his disciples.*
*(Luke 11:1)*

IT WAS OVER TWO thousand years ago that the disciples of Jesus asked Him to teach them to pray. The desire both to know how to pray and to have a prayer life that is satisfying is one that continues to stir in hearts today.

Our Lord lovingly fulfilled the disciples' request when He taught them to pray the Our Father (Luke 11:1–4). By His example, He showed them the necessity of going to a quiet place to pray, to receive guidance and spiritual nourishment (Mark 1:35; Luke 5:16; Matt. 14:23).

While addressing the crowd gathered on the mount, Jesus was likewise reminding the disciples, "When you pray, go into your room and shut the door and pray to your Father who is in secret; and your Father who sees in secret will reward you" (Matt. 6:6).

Archbishop Fulton J. Sheen received this same request that was made of Our Lord: teach us to pray. His students, his parishioners, and his worldwide audience would ask him about ways to pray and about his favorite prayers.

With this in mind, Sheen was keen to encourage people to make prayer a daily, holy habit. To Catholics, he would specifically recommend attending Holy Mass daily whenever possible, to set aside time to pray a Holy Hour, and to pray the Way of the Cross in union with Our Lord's Passion.

Archbishop Fulton J. Sheen was known to have often said: "I do not want my life to be mine. I want it to be Christ's." He had cultivated an intimate prayer life with Christ, and he wanted to share it with everyone.

During the 1930s and '40s, Fulton Sheen was the featured speaker on The Catholic Hour radio broadcast, and millions of listeners heard his radio addresses each week. His topics ranged from politics and the economy to philosophy and man's eternal pursuit of happiness.

Along with his weekly radio program, Sheen wrote dozens of books and pamphlets. One can safely say that through his writings, thousands of people changed their perspectives about God and the Church. Sheen was quoted as saying, "There are not one hundred people in the United States who hate the Catholic Church, but there are millions who hate what they wrongly perceive the Catholic Church to be."

Possessing a burning zeal to dispel the myths about Our Lord and His Church, Sheen gave a series of powerful presentations on Christ's Passion and His seven last words from the Cross. As a Scripture scholar, Archbishop Sheen knew full well the power contained in preaching Christ crucified. With St. Paul, he could say, "For I decided to know nothing among you except Jesus Christ and him crucified" (1 Cor. 2:2).

During his last recorded Good Friday address in 1979, Archbishop Sheen spoke of having given this type of reflection on the subject of Christ's seven last words from the Cross "for the fifty-eighth consecutive time." Whether from the young priest in Peoria, Illinois, the university professor in Washington, D.C., or the bishop in New York, Sheen's messages were sure to make an indelible mark on his listeners.

Given their importance and the impact they had on society, it seemed appropriate to bring back this collection of Sheen's radio addresses that were later compiled into a book titled *Calvary and the Mass* (New York: P.J. Kenedy and Sons, 1936).

In this series of talks, Archbishop Sheen speaks about finding Calvary renewed, re-enacted, and re-presented, in the Mass. Calvary is one with the Mass, and the Mass is one with Calvary, for in both there is the same Priest and Victim. The Seven Last Words are like the seven parts of the Mass. And just as there are seven notes in music admitting an infinite variety of harmonies and combinations, so too on the Cross there are seven divine notes, which the dying Christ rang down the centuries, all of which combine to form the beautiful harmony of the world's redemption.

Each word is a part of the Mass. The First Word, "Forgive," is the Confiteor; the Second Word, "This Day in Paradise," is the Offertory; the Third Word, "Behold Thy Mother," is the Sanctus; the Fourth Word, "Why hast Thou abandoned Me," is the Consecration; the Fifth Word, "I thirst," is the Communion; the Sixth Word, "It is finished," is the Ite, Missa Est; the Seventh Word, "Father, into Thy Hands," is the Last Gospel.

On October 2, 1979, when visiting St. Patrick's Cathedral in New York City, Pope John Paul II embraced Fulton Sheen and spoke into his ear a blessing and an affirmation. He said: "You have written and spoken well of the Lord Jesus Christ. You are a loyal son of the Church." On the day Archbishop Sheen died (December 9, 1979), he was found in his private chapel before the Eucharist in the shadow of the cross. Archbishop Sheen was a man purified in the fires of love and by the wood of the Cross.

It is hoped that, upon reading these reflections, the reader will concur with the heartfelt affirmation given by Pope St. John Paul II about Sheen's giftedness and fidelity. May these writings by Archbishop Fulton J. Sheen evoke a greater love and understanding of the Mass. May they reveal that Cross of Jesus Christ and the Holy Eucharist are two great summits of grace that are available in the world today.

# PROLOGUE

THERE ARE CERTAIN things in life which are too beautiful to be forgotten, such as the love of a mother. Hence we treasure her picture. The love of soldiers who sacrificed themselves for their country is likewise too beautiful to be forgotten; hence, we revere their memory on Memorial Day. But the greatest blessing which ever came to this earth was the visitation of the Son of God in the form and habit of man. His life, above all lives, is too beautiful to be forgotten; hence, we treasure the divinity of His Words in Sacred Scripture and the charity of His Deeds in our daily actions. Unfortunately, this is all some souls remember, namely His Words and His *Deeds*; important as these are, they are not the greatest characteristic of the Divine Saviour.

The most sublime act in the history of Christ was His *Death*. Death is always important for it seals a destiny. Any dying man is a scene. Any dying scene is a sacred place. That is why the great literature of the past, which has touched on the emotions surrounding death, has never passed out of date. But of all deaths in the record of man, none was more important than the Death of Christ. Everyone else, who was ever born into the world, came into it to live; our Lord came into it to die. Death was a stumbling block to the life of Socrates, but it was the crown to the life of Christ. He Himself told us that He came "to give his life redemption for many"; that no one could take away His Life; but He would lay it down of Himself.

If then Death was the supreme moment for which Christ lived, it was, therefore, the one thing He wished to have remembered. He did not ask that men should write down His Words into a Scripture; He did not ask that His kindness to the poor should be recorded in history, but He did ask that men remember His Death. And in order that its memory might not be any haphazard narrative on the part of men, He Himself instituted the precise way it should be recalled.

The memorial was instituted the night before He died, at what has since been called "The Last Supper." Taking bread into His Hands, He said: "This is my body, which shall be delivered for you," i.e., delivered unto death. Then over the chalice of wine, He said, "This is my blood of the new testament, which shall be shed for many unto remission of sins." Thus in an unbloody symbol of the parting of the Blood from the Body, by the separate consecration of Bread and Wine, did Christ pledge Himself to death in the sight of God and men, and represent His death which was to come the next afternoon at three.[1] He was offering Himself as a Victim to be immolated, and that men might never forget that "greater love than this no man hath, that a man lay down his life for his friends." He gave the divine command to the Church: "Do this for a commemoration of me."

The following day, that which He had prefigured and foreshadowed, He realized in its completeness; as He was crucified between two thieves and His Blood drained from His Body for the redemption of the world.

The Church, which Christ founded, has not only preserved the Word He spoke, and the wonders He wrought; it has also taken Him seriously when He said: "Do this for a commemoration of me." And that action whereby we re-enact His Death on the Cross is the Sacrifice of the Mass, in which we do as a memorial what He did at the Last Supper as the prefiguration of His Passion.[2]

Hence the Mass is to us the crowning act of Christian worship. A pulpit in which the words of our Lord are repeated does not unite us to Him; a choir in which sweet sentiments are sung brings us no closer to His Cross than to His garments. A temple without an altar of sacrifice is non-existent among primitive peoples and is meaningless among Christians. And so in the Catholic Church the *altar*, and not the pulpit or the choir or the organ, is the center of worship, for there is re-enacted the memorial of His Passion. Its value does not depend on him who says it, or on him who hears it; it depends on Him who is the One High Priest and Victim, Jesus Christ our Lord. With Him we are united, in spite of our nothingness; in a certain sense, we lose our individuality for the time being; we unite our intellect and our will, our heart and our soul, our body and our blood, so intimately with Christ, that the Heavenly Father sees not so much us with our imperfection, but rather sees us *in Him*, the Beloved Son in whom He is well pleased. The Mass is for that reason the greatest event in the history of mankind; the only Holy Act which keeps the wrath of God from a sinful world, because it holds the Cross between heaven and earth, thus renewing that decisive moment when our sad and tragic humanity journeyed suddenly forth to the fullness of supernatural life.

What is important at this point is that we take the proper mental attitude toward the Mass, and remember this important fact, that the Sacrifice of the Cross is not something which happened two thousand years ago. It is still happening. It is not something past like the signing of the Declaration of Independence; it is an abiding drama on which the curtain has not yet rung down. Let it not be believed that it happened a long time ago, and therefore no more concerns us than anything else in the past. *Calvary belongs to all times and to all places.* That is why, when our Blessed Lord ascended the heights of Calvary, He was fittingly stripped of His garments: He would save the world without the trappings of a passing world. His garments belonged to time, for they localized Him, and fixed Him as a dweller in Galilee. Now that He was shorn of them and utterly dispossessed of earthly things, He belonged not to Galilee, not to a Roman province, but to the world. He became the universal poor man of the world, belonging to no one people, but to all men.

To express further the universality of the Redemption, the cross was erected at the crossroads of civilization, at a central point between the three great cultures of Jerusalem, Rome, and Athens, in whose names He was crucified. The cross was thus placarded before the eyes of men, to arrest the careless, to appeal to the thoughtless, to arouse the worldly. It was the one inescapable fact that the cultures and civilizations of His day could not resist. It is also the one inescapable fact of our day, which we cannot resist.

The figures at the Cross were symbols of all who crucify. We were there in our representatives. What we are doing now to the Mystical Christ, they were doing in our names to the historical Christ. If we are envious of the good, we were there in the Scribes and Pharisees. If we are fearful of losing some temporal advantage by embracing Divine Truth and Love, we were there in Pilate. If we trust in material forces and seek to conquer through the world instead of through the spirit, we were there in Herod. And so the story goes on for the typical sins of the world. They all blind us to the fact that He is God. There was, therefore, a kind of inevitability about the Crucifixion. Men who were free to sin were also free to crucify.

As long as there is sin in the world, the Crucifixion is a reality. As the poet Rachel Annand Taylor has put it:


"I saw the son of man go by,
Crowned with a crown of thorns.
'Was it not finished Lord,' said I,
'And all the anguish borne?'

He turned on me His awful eyes;
'Hast Thou not understood?
So every soul is a Calvary
And every sin a rood.'"

We were there then during that Crucifixion. The drama was already completed as far as the vision of Christ was concerned, but it had not yet been unfolded to all men and all places and all times. If a motion picture reel, for example, were conscious of itself, it would know the drama from beginning to end, but the spectators in the theater would not know it until they had seen it unrolled upon the screen. In like manner, our Lord on the Cross saw His eternal mind, the whole drama of history, the story of each individual soul and how later on it would react to His Crucifixion; but though He saw all, we could not know how we would react to the Cross until we were unrolled upon the screen of time. We were not conscious of being present there on Calvary that day, but He was conscious of our presence. Today we know the role we played in the theater of Calvary, by the way, we live and act now in the theater of the twentieth century.

That is why Calvary is actual; why the Cross is the Crisis; why in a certain sense the scars are still open; why Pain still stands deified, and why blood like falling stars is still dropping upon our souls. There is no escaping the Cross, not even by denying it as the Pharisees did; not even by selling Christ as Judas did; not even by crucifying Him as the executioners did. We all see it, either to embrace it in salvation or to fly from it into misery.

But how is it made visible? Where shall we find Calvary perpetuated? We shall find Calvary renewed, re-enacted, re-presented, as we have seen, in the Mass. Calvary is one with the Mass, and the Mass is one with Calvary, for in both there is the same Priest and Victim. The Seven Last Words are like the seven parts of the Mass. And just as there are seven notes in music admitting an infinite variety of harmonies and combinations, so too on the Cross there are seven divine notes, which the dying Christ rang down the centuries, all of which combine to form the beautiful harmony of the world's redemption.

Each word is a part of the Mass. The First Word, "Forgive," is the Confiteor; the Second Word, "This Day in Paradise," is the Offertory; the Third Word, "Behold Thy Mother," is the Sanctus; the Fourth Word, "Why hast Thou abandoned Me," is the Consecration; the Fifth Word, "I thirst," is the Communion; the Sixth

Word, "It is finished," is the Ite, Missa Est; the Seventh Word, "Father, into Thy Hands," is the Last Gospel.

Picture then the High Priest Christ leaving the sacristy of heaven for the altar of Calvary. He has already put on the vestment of our human nature, the maniple of our suffering, the stole of priesthood, the chasuble of the Cross. Calvary is his cathedral; the rock of Calvary is the altar stone; the sun turning to red is the sanctuary lamp; Mary and John are the living side altars; the Host is His Body; the wine is His Blood. He is upright as Priest, yet He is prostrate as Victim. His Mass is about to begin.

(1) "Death is put before us in a symbol, by means of that sacramental parting of the Blood from the Body; but death at the same time already pledged to God for all its worth, as well as all its awful reality, by the expressive language of the Sacred Symbol. The price of our sins shall be paid down on Calvary, but here the liability is incurred by our Redeemer and subscribed in His very Blood"-Maurice de la Taille, S.J.-Catholic Faith in the Holy Eucharist, p. 115. "There were not two distinct and complete sacrifices offered by Christ, one in the Cenacle, the other on Calvary. There was a sacrifice at the Last Supper, but it was the sacrifice of Redemption, and there was a sacrifice on the Cross, but it was the selfsame sacrifice continued and completed. The Supper and the Cross made up one complete sacrifice."- Maurice de la Taille, S.J., The Mystery of Faith and Human Opinion, p. 232.

(2) "He offered the Victim to be immolated; we offer it as immolated of old. We offer the eternal Victim of the Cross, once made and forever enduring... The Mass is a sacrifice because it is our oblation of the Victim once immolated, even as the Supper was the oblation of the Victim to be immolated." ibid. p. 239-240. The Mass is not only a commemoration; it is a living representation of the sacrifice of the cross. "In this Divine Sacrifice, which takes place at the Mass is contained and immolated, in an unbloody manner, the same Christ that was offered once for all in the blood upon the Cross ... It is one and the same Victim, one and the same High Priest, who made the offering through the ministry of His priests today, after having offered Himself upon the cross yesterday; only the manner of the oblation is different" (Council of Trent, Session 22).

# THE CONFITEOR

*"Father, forgive them,*

*for they know not what they do."*

THE MASS BEGINS with the Confiteor. The Confiteor is a prayer in which we confess our sins and ask the Blessed Mother and the saints to intercede to God for our forgiveness, for only the clean of heart can see God. Our Blessed Lord also begins His Mass with the Confiteor. But His Confiteor differs from ours in this: He has no sins to confess. He is God and therefore, is sinless. "Which of you shall convince me of sin?" His Confiteor then cannot be a prayer for the forgiveness of *His* sins, but it can be a prayer for the forgiveness of our sins.

Others would have screamed, cursed, wrestled, as the nails pierced their hands and feet. But no vindictiveness finds place in the Saviour's breast; no appeal comes from His lips for vengeance on His murderers; He breathes no prayer for strength to bear His pain. Incarnate Love forgets injury, forgets pain, and in that moment of concentrated agony reveals something of the height, the depth, and the breadth of the wonderful love of God, as He says His Confiteor: "Father, forgive them, for they know not what they do."

He did not say, "Forgive Me," but "Forgive them." The moment of death was certainly the one most likely to produce confession of sin, for conscience in the last solemn hours does assert its authority; and yet not a single sigh of penitence escaped His lips. He was associated with sinners but never associated with sin. In death as well as life, He was unconscious of a single unfulfilled duty to His heavenly Father. And why? Because a sinless Man is not just a man; He is more than mere man. He is sinless because He is God – and there is the difference. We draw our prayers from the depths of our consciousness of sin: He drew His silence from His own intrinsic sinlessness. That one word, "Forgive" proves Him to be the Son of God.

Notice the grounds on which He asked His heavenly Father to forgive us – "Because they know not what they do." When anyone injures us or blames us wrongly, we say: "They should have known better." But when we sin against God, He finds an excuse for forgiveness – our ignorance.

There is no redemption for the fallen angels. The blood drops that fell from the cross on Good Friday in that Mass of Christ did not touch the spirits of the fallen angels. Why? Because they knew what they were doing? They saw all the consequences of their acts, just as clearly as we see that two and two make four, or that a thing cannot exist and not exist at the same time. Truths of this kind when understood cannot be taken back; they are irrevocable and eternal. Hence when they decided to rebel against Almighty God, there was no taking back the decision. They knew what they were doing!

But with us it is different. We do not see the consequences of our acts as clearly as the angels; we are weaker; we are ignorant. But if we did know that every sin of pride wove a crown of thorns for the head of Christ; if we knew that every contradiction of His divine command made for Him the sign of contradiction, the Cross; if we knew that every grasping avaricious act nailed His hands, and every journey into the byways of sin dug His feet; if we knew how good God is and still went on sinning, we would never be saved. It is only our ignorance of the infinite love of the Sacred Heart that brings us within the hearing of His Confiteor from the Cross: "Father, forgive them, for they know not what they do."

These words, let it be deeply graven on our souls, do not constitute an excuse for continued sin, but a motive for contrition and penance. Forgiveness is not a denial of sin. Our Lord does not deny the horrible fact of sin, and that is where the modern world is wrong. It explains sin away: it ascribes it to a fall in the evolutionary process, to a survival of ancient taboos; it identifies it with psychological verbiage.

In a word, the modern world denies sin. Our Lord reminds us that it is the most terrible of all realities. Otherwise, why does it give Sinlessness a cross? Why does it shed innocent blood? Why does it have such awful associations: blindness, compromise, cowardice, hatred, and cruelty? Why does it now lift itself out of the realm of the impersonal and assert itself as personal by nailing Innocence to a gibbet? An abstraction cannot do that. But sinful man can.

Hence He, who loved men unto death, allowed sin to wreak its vengeance upon Him, in order that they might forever understand its horror as the crucifixion of Him who loved them most.

There is no denial of sin here – and yet, with all its horror, the Victim forgives. In that one and the same event, there is the sign of sin's utter depravity and the seal of divine forgiveness. From that point on, no man can look upon a crucifix and say that sin is not serious, nor can he ever say that it cannot be forgiven. By the way He suffered, He revealed the reality of sin; by the way, He bore it, He shows His mercy toward the sinner.

It is the Victim who has suffered that forgives: and in that combination of a Victim so humanly beautiful, so divinely loving, so wholly innocent, does one find a Great Crime and a Greater Forgiveness. Under the shelter of the Blood of Christ, the worst sinners may take their stand; for there is a power in that Blood to turn back the tides of vengeance which threaten to drown the world.

The world will give you sin explained away, but only on Calvary do you experience the divine contradiction of sin forgiven. On the Cross, supreme self-giving and divine love transforms sin's worst act in the noblest deed and sweetest prayer the world has ever seen or heard, the Confiteor of Christ: "Father, forgive them, for they know not what they do."

That word "Forgive," which rang out from the Cross that day when sin rose to its full strength and then fell defeated by Love, did not die with its echo. Not long before, that same merciful Saviour had taken means to prolong forgiveness through space and time, even to the consummation of the world. Gathering the nucleus of His Church round about Him, He said to His Apostles: "Whose sins you shall forgive, they are forgiven."

Somewhere in the world today then, the successors of the Apostles have the power to forgive. It is not for us to ask: But how can man forgive sins? – For man cannot forgive sins. But God can forgive sins *through* man, for is not that the way God forgave His executioners on the cross, namely through the instrumentality of His human nature?

Why then is it not reasonable to expect Him still to forgive sins through other human natures to whom He gave that power? And where find those human natures?

You know the story of the box, which was long ignored and even ridiculed as worthless; and one day it was opened and found to contain the great heart of a giant. In every Catholic Church, that box exists. We call it the confessional box. It is ignored and ridiculed by many, but in it is to be found the Sacred Heart of the forgiving Christ, forgiving sinners through the uplifted hand of His priest, as He once forgave through His own uplifted hands on the Cross. There is only one forgiveness – the Forgiveness of God. There is only one 'Forgive'

– the 'Forgive' of an eternal Divine Act in which we come in contact at various moments of time.

As the air is always filled with symphony and speech, but we do not hear it unless we tune it in on our radios, so neither do souls feel the joy of that eternal and divine 'Forgive' unless they are attuned to it in time; and the confessional box is the place where we tune in to that cry from the Cross.

Would to God that our modern mind instead of denying the guilt, would look to the Cross, admit its guilt, and seek forgiveness; would that those who have uneasy consciences that worry them in the light and haunt them in the darkness, would seek relief, not on the plane of medicine but on the plane of Divine Justice; would that they who tell the dark secrets of their minds, would do so not for the sake of sublimation, but for the sake of purgation; would that those poor mortals who shed tears in silence would find an absolving hand to wipe them away.

Must it be forever true that the greatest tragedy of life is not what happens to souls, but rather what souls miss? And what greater tragedy is there than to miss the peace of sin forgiven? The Confiteor is at the foot of the altar our cry of unworthiness: the Confiteor from the Cross is our hope of pardon and absolution. The wounds of the Saviour were terrible, but the worst wound of all would be to be unmindful that we caused it all. The Confiteor can save us from that, for it is an admission that there is something to be forgiven – and more than we shall ever know.

There is a story told of a nun who was one day dusting a small image of Our Blessed Lord in the chapel. In the course of her duty, she let it slip to the floor. She picked it up undamaged, she kissed it, and put it back again in its place, saying, "If you had never fallen, you never would have received that." I wonder if our Blessed Lord does not feel the same way about us, for if we had never sinned, we never could call Him "Saviour."

# THE OFFERTORY

*"Amen I say to thee, this day thou*

*shalt be with me in paradise."*

THIS IS NOW THE offertory of the Mass, for our Lord is offering Himself to His heavenly Father. But in order to remind us that He is not offered alone, but in union with us, He unites with His offertory the soul of the thief at the right. To make His ignominy more complete, in a masterstroke of malice, they crucified Him between two thieves. He walked among sinners during His life, so now they let Him hang between them at death. But He changed the picture and made the two thieves the symbols of the sheep and the goats, which will stand at His right and left hand when He comes in the clouds of heaven, with His then triumphant cross, to judge both the living and the dead.

Both thieves at first reviled and blasphemed, but one of them, whom tradition calls Dismas, turned his head to read the meekness and dignity on the face of the crucified Saviour. As a piece of coal thrown into the fire is transformed into a bright and glowing thing, so the black soul of this thief thrown into the fires of the Crucifixion glowed with love for the Sacred Heart.

While the thief on the left was saying: "If thou be Christ, save thyself and us," the repentant thief rebuked him saying: "Neither dost thou fear God, seeing thou art under the same condemnation. And we indeed justly, for we receive the due reward of our deeds; but this man hath done no evil." That same thief then emitted a plea, not for a place in the seats of the mighty, but only not to be forgotten: "Remember me, when thou shalt come into thy kingdom."

Such sorrow and faith must not go unrewarded. At a moment when the power of Rome could not make Him speak when His friends thought all was lost, and His enemies believed all was won, our Lord broke the silence. He, who was the accused, became the Judge: He, who was the crucified, became the Divine Assessor of souls. As to the penitent thief, He trumpeted the words: "This day thou shalt be with me in paradise." This day – when you said your first prayer and your last; this day – thou shalt be with me – and where I am, there is paradise.

With these words our Lord who was offering Himself to His heavenly Father as the great Host, now unites with Him on the paten of the cross the first small host ever offered in the Mass, the host of the repentant thief, a brand plucked from the burning, a sheaf torn from the earthly reapers; the wheat ground in the mill of the crucifixion and made bread for the Eucharist.

Our Lord does not suffer alone on the Cross: He suffers with us. That is why He united the sacrifice of the thief with His own. It is this St. Paul means when he says that we should fill up those things that are wanting to the sufferings of Christ. This does not mean our Lord on the cross did not suffer all He could. It means rather that the physical, historical Christ suffered all He could in His own human nature, but that the Mystical Christ, which is Christ and us, has not suffered to *our* fullness. All the other good thieves in the history of the world have not yet admitted their wrong and pleaded for remembrances. Our Lord is now in heaven. He, therefore, can suffer no more in His human nature, but He can suffer more in our human natures.

So He reaches out to other human natures, to yours and mine, and asks us to do as the thief did, namely, to incorporate ourselves to Him on the Cross, that sharing in His Crucifixion we might also share in His Resurrection, and that made partakers of His Cross we might also be made partakers of His glory in heaven.

As our Blessed Lord on that day chose the thief as the small host of sacrifice, He chooses us today as the other small hosts united with Him on the paten of the altar. Go back in your mind's eye to a Mass, to any Mass which was celebrated in the first centuries of the Church, before civilization became completely financial and economic. If we went to the Holy Sacrifice in the early Church, we would have brought to the altar each morning some bread and some wine. The priest would have used one piece of that unleavened bread and some of that wine for the sacrifice of the Mass. The rest would have been put aside, blessed, and distributed to the poor. Today we do not bring bread and wine. We bring its equivalent: we bring that which buys bread and wine. Hence the offertory collection.

Why do we bring bread and wine or its equivalent to the Mass? We bring bread and wine because these two things, of all things in nature, most represent the substance of life. Wheat is as the very marrow of the ground, and the grapes its very blood, both of which give us the body and blood of life. In bringing those two things, which give us life, nourish us, *we are equivalently bringing ourselves to* the Sacrifice of the Mass.

We are therefore present at each and every Mass under the appearance of bread and wine, which stand as symbols of our body and blood. We are not passive spectators as we might be watching a spectacle in a theater, but we are co-offering our Mass with Christ. If any picture adequately describes our role in this drama, it is this: There is a great cross before us on which is stretched the great Host, Christ. Round about the hill of Calvary are our small crosses on which we, the small hosts, are to be offered. When our Lord goes to His Cross, we go to our little crosses, and offer ourselves in union with Him, as a clean oblation to the heavenly Father.

At that moment we literally fulfill to the smallest detail the Saviour's command: Take up your cross daily and follow Me. In doing so, He is not asking us to do anything He has not already done Himself. Nor is it any excuse to say: "I am a poor unworthy host." So was the thief.

Note that there were two attitudes in the soul of that thief, both of which made him acceptable to our Lord. The first was the recognition of the fact that He deserved what He was suffering, but that the sinless Christ did not deserve His Cross; in other words, he was *penitent*. The second was *faith* in Him whom men rejected, but whom the thief recognized as the very King of Kings.

Upon what conditions do we become small hosts in the Mass? How does our sacrifice become one with Christ's and as acceptable as the thief's? Only by reproducing in our souls the two attitudes in the soul of the thief: *penitence* and *faith*.

First of all, we must be penitent with the thief and say: "I deserve punishment for my sins. I stand in need of sacrifice." Some of us do not know how wicked or how ungrateful to God we are. If we did, we would not so complain about the shocks and pains of life. Our consciences are like darkened rooms from which light has been long excluded. We draw the curtain and lo! Everywhere what we thought was cleanliness, we now find dust.

Some consciences have been so filmed over with excuses that they pray with the Pharisee: "I thank Thee, O God, that I am not as the rest of men." Others blaspheme the God of heaven for their pain and sins but repent not. The World War, for example, was meant to be a purgation of evil; it was meant to teach us that we cannot get along without God, but the world refused to learn the lesson. Like the thief on the left, it refuses to be penitent: it refuses to see any relation of justice between sin and sacrifice, between rebellion and a cross.

But the more penitent we are, the less anxious we are to escape our cross. The more we see ourselves as we are, the more we say with the good thief: "I deserved this cross." He did not want to be excused; he did not want to have his sin explained away; he did not want to be let off; he did not ask to be taken down. He wanted only to be forgiven. He was willing even to be a small host on his own little cross – but that was because he was penitent. Nor is there given to us any other way to become little hosts with Christ in the Mass than by breaking our hearts with sorrow; for unless we admit we are wounded how can we feel the need of healing? Unless we are sorry for our part in the Crucifixion, how could we ever ask to be forgiven its sin?

The second condition of becoming a host in the offertory of the Mass is faith. The thief looked above the head of our Blessed Lord and saw a sign which read: "KING." Strange king that! For a crown: thorns. For royal purple: His own blood. For a throne: a cross. For courtiers: executioners. For a coronation: a crucifixion.

And yet beneath all that dross, the thief saw the gold; amidst all those blasphemies he prayed.

His faith was so strong he was content to remain on his cross. The thief on the left asked to be taken down, but not the thief on the right. Why? Because he knew there were greater evils than crucifixions and another life beyond the cross. He had faith in the Man on the central cross who could have turned thorns into garlands and nails into rosebuds if He willed; but he had faith in a Kingdom beyond the cross, knowing that the sufferings of this world are not worthy to be compared with the joys that are to come. With the Psalmist, his soul cried: "Though I should walk in the midst of the shadow of death, I will fear no evils, for thou art with me."

Such faith was like that of the three youths in the fiery furnace who were commanded by the king, Nebuchadnezzar, to adore the golden statue. Their answer was: "For behold, our God, whom we worship, is able to save us from the furnace of burning fire, and to deliver us out of thy hands, O king. But if He will not, be it known to thee, O king, that we will not worship thy gods, nor adore the golden statue which thou hast set up." Note that they did not ask God to deliver them from the fiery furnace, though they knew God could do it, "for He is

able to save us from the furnace of burning fire."
They left themselves wholly in God's hands, and
like Job, they trusted Him.

So likewise, with the good thief: He knew
our Lord could deliver Him. But *he did not ask
to be taken down from the cross*, for our Lord
did not come down Himself even though the
mob challenged Him. The thief would be a
small host, if need be, unto the very end of the
Mass. This did not mean the thief did not love
life: He loved life as much as we love it. He
wanted life and a long life, and he found it, for
what life is longer than Life Eternal. To each
and every one of us in like manner, it is given to
discover that Eternal Life. But there is no other
way to enter it than by penance and by faith,
which unite us to that Great Host – the Priest
and Victim Christ. Thus do we become spiritual
thieves and steal heaven once again.

# THE SANCTUS

*"Woman, behold thy son . . .*

*behold thy mother."*

FIVE DAYS AGO OUR Blessed Lord made a triumphal entry into the city of Jerusalem: Triumphant cries rang about His ears; palms dropped beneath His feet, as the air resounded with hosannas to the Son of David and praises to the Holy One of Israel. To those who would have silenced the demonstration in His honour, our Lord reminds them that if their voices were silent, even the very stones would have cried out. That was the birthday of Gothic cathedrals.

They did not know the real reason why they were calling Him *holy*; they did not even understand why He accepted the tribute of their praise. They thought that they were proclaiming Him a kind of earthly king. But He accepted their demonstration because He was going to be the King of a spiritual empire. He accepted their tributes, their hosannas, and their pæans of praise because He was going to His cross as a Victim. And every victim must be holy – *Sanctus, Sanctus, Sanctus*. Five days later came the *Sanctus* of the Mass of Calvary. But at that *Sanctus* of His Mass, He does not say "holy" – He speaks to the holy ones; He does not whisper "Sanctus" – He addresses Himself *to* saints, to His sweet Mother Mary, and His beloved disciple, John.

Striking words they are: "Woman, behold thy son . . . behold thy mother." He was speaking now to saints. He had no need of saintly intercession, for He was the Holy One of God. But we have need of holiness, for every victim of the Mass must be holy, undefiled, and unpolluted. But how can we be holy participants in the Sacrifice of the Mass? He gave the answer: namely, by putting ourselves under the protection of His Blessed Mother. He addresses the Church and all its members in the person of John, and says to each of us: "Behold thy mother." That is why He addressed her not as "Mother" but as "Woman." She had a universal mission, to be not only His Mother but to be the Mother of all Christians. She had been His Mother; now, she was to be the Mother of His Mystical Body, the Church. And we were to be her children.

There is a tremendous mystery hidden in that one word, "Woman." It was really the last lesson in detachment which Jesus had been teaching her these many years and the first lesson of the new attachment. Our Lord had been gradually 'alienating,' as it were, His affections from His Mother, not in the sense that she was to love Him less, or that He was to love her less but only in the sense that she was to love us more. She was to be detached from motherhood in the flesh, only to be more attached to that greater motherhood in the spirit. Hence the word: "Woman." She was to make us *other Christs*, for as Mary had raised the Holy One of God, so only she could raise us as holy ones for God, worthy to say *Sanctus, Sanctus, Sanctus*, in the Mass of that prolonged Calvary.

The story of the preparation for her role as Mother of the Mystical Body of Christ is unfolded in three scenes in the life of her divine Son, each one suggesting the lesson which Calvary itself was to reveal: namely, that she was called to be not only the Mother of God but also the Mother of men; not only the Mother of holiness but the Mother of those who ask to be holy.

The first scene took place in the Temple, where Mary and Joseph found Jesus after a three-day search. The Blessed Mother reminds Him that their hearts were broken with sorrow during the long search, and He answers: "Did you not know that I must be about my Father's business?" Here He was equivalently saying: "I have another business, Mother, than the business of the carpenter shop. My Father has sent Me into this world on the supreme business of Redemption, to make all men adopted sons of My heavenly Father in the greater kingdom of the brotherhood of Christ, Thy Son." How far the full vision of those words dawned upon Mary, we know not; whether she then understood that the Fatherhood of God meant that she was to be the Mother of men, we know not. But certainly, eighteen years later, in the second scene, the marriage feast of Cana, she came to a fuller understanding of that mission.

What a consoling thought it is to think that our Blessed Lord, who talked penance, who preached mortification, who insisted upon taking up the cross daily and following Him, should have begun His public life by assisting at a wedding festival! What a beautiful understanding of our hearts!

When in the course of the banquet, the wine was exhausted, Mary, always interested in others, was the first to notice, and the first to seek relief from the embarrassment. She simply said to our Blessed Lord, "They have no wine." And our Blessed Lord said to her, "Woman, what is that to me and to thee? my hour is not yet come." "Woman, what is that to me?" He did not call her "Mother," but "Woman" – the same title she was to receive three years later.

He was equivalently saying to her: "You are asking Me to do something which belongs to Me as the Son of God. You are asking Me to work a miracle which only God can work; you are asking Me to exercise My divinity, which has relationship to all mankind, namely as its Redeemer. But once that divinity operates for the salvation of the world, you become not only My Mother but the Mother of redeemed humanity. Your physical motherhood passes into the wider world of spiritual motherhood, and for that reason, I call you: 'Woman.'" And in order to prove that her intercession is powerful in that role of universal motherhood, He ordered the pots filled with water, and in the language of Crashaw the first miracle was worked: "the conscious waters saw their God and blushed."

The third scene happens within two years. One day as our Lord was preaching someone interrupted His discourse to say, "Thy mother . . . stands without, seeking thee." Our Blessed Lord said, "Who is my mother?" and stretching forth His hands toward His disciples He said: "Behold my mother and my brethren.

For whosoever shall do the will of my Father, that is in heaven, he is my brother, and my sister, and mother." The meaning was unmistakable. There is such a thing as spiritual maternity; there are bonds other than those of the flesh; there are ties other than the ties of blood, namely spiritual ties which band together those of the Kingdom where reign the Fatherhood of God and the Brotherhood of Christ.

These three scenes have their climax at the Cross, where Mary is called "Woman." It was the second Annunciation. The angel said to her in the first: "Hail, Mary." Her Son speaks to her in the second: "Woman." This did not mean she ceased to be His Mother; she is always the Mother of God; but her Motherhood enlarged and expanded; it became spiritual, it became universal, for at that moment she became our mother. Our Lord created the bond where it did not exist by nature as only He could do.

And how did she become the Mother of men? By becoming not only the mother but also the spouse of Christ. He was the new Adam; she is the new Eve. And as Adam and Eve brought forth their natural progeny, which we are, so Christ and His Mother brought forth at the Cross their spiritual progeny, which we are: children of Mary or members of the Mystical

Body of Christ. She brought forth her First-born at Bethlehem. Note that St. Luke calls our Lord the *First-born* – not that our Blessed Mother was to have other children *according to the flesh*, but only because she was to have other children *according to the spirit*. That moment when our Blessed Lord said to her, "Woman," she became in a certain sense the spouse of Christ, and she brought forth in sorrow her first-born in the spirit, and his name was John. Who the second-born was we know not. It might have been Peter. It might have been Andrew. But we, at any rate, are the millionth-and-millionth-born of that woman at the foot of the Cross. It was a poor exchange indeed, receiving the son of Zebedee in place of the Son of God. But surely our gain was greater, for while she acquired but undutiful and often rebellious children, we obtained the most loving Mother in the world – the Mother of Jesus.

We are children of Mary – literally, *children*. She is our Mother, not by title of fiction, not by title of courtesy; she is our Mother because she endured at that particular moment the pains of childbirth for all of us. And why did our Lord give her to us as Mother? Because He knew *we could never be holy without her*. He came to us through her purity, and only through her purity can we go back to her. There is no Sanctus apart from Mary. Every victim that mounts that altar under the species of bread and wine must have said the Confiteor, and become a holy victim – but there is no holiness without Mary.

Note that when that word was spoken to our Blessed Mother, there was another woman there who was prostrate. Have you ever remarked that practically every traditional representation of the Crucifixion always pictures Magdalene on her knees at the foot of the crucifix? But you have never yet seen an image of the Blessed Mother prostrate. John was there, and he tells in his Gospel that she stood. He saw her stand. But why did she stand? She stood to be of service to us. She stood to be our minister, our Mother.

If Mary could have prostrated herself at that moment as Magdalene did, if she could have only wept, her sorrow would have had an outlet. The sorrow that cries is never the sorrow that breaks the heart. It is the heart that can find no outlet in the fountain of tears which cracks; it is the heart that cannot have an emotional break-down that breaks. And all that sorrow was part of our purchase price paid by our Co-Redemptrix, Mary the Mother of God!

Because our Lord willed her to us as our Mother, He left her on this earth after He ascended into heaven, in order that she might mother the infant Church. The infant Church had need of a mother, just as the infant Christ. She had to remain on earth until her family had grown. That is why we find her on Pentecost abiding in prayer with the Apostles, awaiting the descent of the Holy Spirit. She was mothering the Mystical Body of Christ.

Now she is crowned in heaven as Queen of Angels and Saints, turning heaven into another marriage feast of Cana when she intercedes with her divine Saviour on behalf of us, her other children, brothers of Christ and sons of the heavenly Father.

Virgin Mother! What a beautiful conjunction of virginity and motherhood, one supplying the defect of the other. Virginity alone lacks something: there is an incompleteness about it; something unfulfilled; a faculty unused. Motherhood alone loses something: there is a surrender, an unflowering, a plucking of a blossom. Oh! For a *rapprochement* in which there would be a virginity that never lacked anything and a motherhood that never lost anything! We have both in Mary, the Virgin Mother: Virgin by the overshadowing of the Holy Spirit in Bethlehem and Pentecost; Mother by the millions of her progeny from Jesus unto you and me.

There is no question here of confusing our Lady and our Lord; we venerate our Mother, we worship our Lord. We ask of Jesus those things which only God can give: mercy, grace, and forgiveness. We ask that Mary should intercede for us with Him, and especially at the hour of our death. Because of her nearness to Jesus, which her vocation involves, we know our Lord listens especially to her appeal. To no other saint can we speak as a child to its mother: no other virgin, or martyr, or mother, or confessor has ever suffered as much for us as she has; no one has ever established better claim to our love and patronage than she.

As the Mediatrix of all graces, all favors come to us from Jesus through her, as Jesus himself came to us through her. We wish to be holy, but we know there is no holiness without her, for she was the gift of Jesus to us at the *Sanctus* of His Cross. No woman can ever forget the child of her womb; then certainly Mary can never forget us. That is why we feel way down deep in our hearts that every time she sees another innocent child at the First Communion rail, or another penitent sinner making his way to the Cross, or another broken heart pleading that the water of a wasted life be changed into the wine of God's love, that she hears once again that word: "Woman, behold thy son."

# THE CONSECRATION

*"My God, My God,*

*why hast thou forsaken me?"*

THE FOURTH WORD is the Consecration of the Mass of Calvary. The first three Words were spoken to men, but the last four Words were spoken to God. We are now in the final stage of the Passion. In the fourth Word, in all the universe, there is but God and Himself. This is the hour of darkness. Suddenly out of its blackness, the silence is broken by a cry – so terrible, so unforgettable, that even those who did not understand the dialect remembered the strange tones: *"Eli, Eli, lamma sabacthani."* They recorded it so, a rough rendering of the Hebrew because they could never get the sound of those tones out of their ears all the days of their life.

The darkness, which was covering the earth at that moment, was only the external symbol of the dark night of the soul within. Well indeed might the sun hide its face, at the terrible crime of Deicide. A real reason why the earth was made was to have a Cross erected upon it. And now that the Cross was erected, creation felt the pain and went into darkness.

But why the cry of darkness? Why the cry of abandonment: "My God, my God, why hast thou forsaken me?" It was the cry of atonement for sin. Sin is the abandonment of God by man; it is the creature forsaking the Creator, as a flower might abandon the sunlight, which gave its strength and beauty. Sin is a separation, a divorce – the original divorce from unity with God, whence all other divorces are derived.

Since He came on earth to redeem men from sin, it was therefore fitting that He *feels* that abandonment, that separation, that divorce. He felt it first internally, in His soul, as the base of a mountain, if conscious, might feel abandoned by the sun when a cloud drifted about it, even though its great heights were radiant with light. There was no sin in His soul, but since He willed to feel the effect of sin, an awful sense of isolation and loneliness crept over Him – the loneliness of being without God.

Surrendering the divine consolation which might have been His, He sank into an awful human aloneness, to atone for the solitariness of a soul that has lost God by sin; for the loneliness of the atheist who says there is no God, for the isolation of the man who gives up his faith for things, and for the broken-heartedness of all sinners who are homesick without God. He even went so far as to redeem all those who will not trust, who in sorrow and misery curse and abandon God, crying out: "Why this death? Why should I lose my property? Why should I suffer?" He atoned for all these things by asking a "Why" of God.

But in order better to reveal the intensity of that feeling of abandonment, He revealed it by an external sign. Because man had separated himself from God, He, in atonement, permitted His Blood to be separated from His Body. Sin had entered into the blood of man; and as if the sins of the world were upon Him, He drained the chalice of His Body of His sacred Blood. We can almost hear Him say: "Father, this is My Body; this is My Blood. They are being separated from one another as humanity has been separated from Thee. This is the consecration of My Cross."

What happened there on the Cross that day is happening now in the Mass, with this difference: On the Cross the Saviour was alone; in the Mass, He is with us. Our Lord is now in heaven at the right hand of the Father, making intercession for us. He, therefore, can never suffer again *in His own human nature*. How then can the Mass be the re-enactment of

Calvary? How can Christ renew the Cross? He cannot suffer again in His own human nature, which is in heaven enjoying beatitude, but He can suffer again in our human natures. He cannot renew Calvary in His *physical body*, but He can renew it in *His Mystical Body* – the Church. The Sacrifice of the Cross can be re-enacted provided we give Him our body and our blood, and give it to Him so completely that as His own, He can offer Himself anew to His heavenly Father for the redemption of His Mystical Body, the Church.

So the Christ goes out into the world gathering up other human natures who are willing to be Christs. In order that our sacrifices, our sorrows, our Golgothas, our crucifixions, may not be isolated, disjointed, and unconnected, the Church collects them, harvests them, unifies them, coalesces them, masses them, and this massing of all our sacrifices of our individual human natures is united with the Great Sacrifice of Christ on the Cross in the Mass.

When we assist at the Mass we are not just individuals of the earth or solitary units, but living parts of a great spiritual order in which the Infinite penetrates and enfolds the finite, the Eternal breaks into the temporal, and the Spiritual clothes itself in the garments of materiality. Nothing more solemn exists on the face of God's earth than the awe-inspiring moment of Consecration; for the Mass is not a prayer, nor a hymn, nor something said – it is a Divine Act with which we come in contact at a given moment of time.

An imperfect illustration may be drawn from the radio. The air is filled with symphonies and speech. We do not put the words or music there; but, if we choose, we may establish contact with them by tuning in our radio. And so with the Mass. It is a singular, unique Divine Act with which we come in contact each time it is re-presented and re-enacted in the Mass.

When the die of a medal or coin is struck, the medal is the material, visible representation of a spiritual idea existing in the mind of the artist. Countless reproductions may be made from that original as each new piece of metal is brought in contact with it, and impressed by it. Despite the multiplicity of coins made, the pattern is always the same. In like manner in the Mass, the Pattern – Christ's sacrifice on Calvary – is renewed on our altars as each human being is brought in contact with it at the moment of consecration; but the sacrifice is one and the same despite the multiplicity of Masses. The Mass then is the communication of the

Sacrifice of Calvary to us under the species of bread and wine.

We are on the altar under the appearance of bread and wine, for both are the sustenance of life; therefore, in giving that which gives us life we are symbolically giving ourselves. Furthermore, wheat must suffer to become bread; grapes must pass through the winepress to become wine. Hence both are representative of Christians who are called to suffer with Christ, that they may also reign with Him.

As the consecration of the Mass draws near our Lord is equivalently saying to us: "You, Mary; you, John; you, Peter; and you, Andrew – you, all of you – give Me your body; give Me your blood. Give Me your whole self! I can suffer no more. I have passed through My cross, I have filled up the sufferings of My physical body, but I have not filled up the sufferings wanting to My Mystical Body, in which you are. The Mass is the moment when each one of you may literally fulfill My injunction: 'Take up your cross and follow Me.'"

On the cross, our Blessed Lord was looking forward to you, hoping that one day you would be giving yourself to Him at the moment of consecration. Today, in the Mass, that hope our Blessed Lord entertained for you is fulfilled.

When you assist at the Mass, He expects you now actually to give Him yourself.

Then as the moment of consecration arrives, the priest in obedience to the words of our Lord, "Do this for a commemoration of me," takes bread in his hands and says, "This is my body"; and then over the chalice of wine says, "This is the chalice of my blood of the new and eternal testament." He does not consecrate the bread and wine together, but separately. The separate consecration of the bread and wine is a symbolic representation of the separation of body and blood, and since the Crucifixion entailed that very mystery, Calvary is thus renewed on our altar. But Christ, as has been said, is not alone on our altar; we are with Him. Hence the words of consecration have a double sense; the primary signification of the words is: "This is the Body of Christ; this is the Blood of Christ;" but the secondary signification is "This is my body; this is my blood."

Such is the purpose of life! To redeem ourselves in union with Christ; to apply His merits to our souls by being like Him in all things, even to His death on the Cross. He passed through His consecration on the Cross that we might now pass through ours in the Mass. There is nothing more tragic in all the world than wasted pain.

Think of how much suffering there is in hospitals, among the poor, and the bereaved. Think also of how much of that suffering goes to waste! How many of those lonesome, suffering, abandoned, crucified souls are saying with our Lord at the moment of consecration, "This is my body. Take it," And yet that is what we all should be saying at that second:

I GIVE MYSELF TO GOD. HERE IS MY BODY. TAKE IT. HERE IS MY BLOOD. TAKE IT. HERE IS MY SOUL, MY WILL, MY ENERGY, MY STRENGTH, MY PROPERTY, MY WEALTH – ALL THAT I HAVE. IT IS YOURS. TAKE IT! CONSECRATE IT! OFFER IT! OFFER IT WITH THYSELF TO THE HEAVENLY FATHER IN ORDER THAT HE, LOOKING DOWN ON THIS GREAT SACRIFICE, MAY SEE ONLY THEE, HIS BELOVED SON, IN WHOM HE IS WELL PLEASED. TRANSMUTE THE POOR BREAD OF MY LIFE INTO THY DIVINE LIFE; THRILL THE WINE OF MY WASTED LIFE INTO THY DIVINE SPIRIT; UNITE MY BROKEN HEART WITH THY HEART; CHANGE MY CROSS INTO A CRUCIFIX. LET NOT MY ABANDONMENT, AND MY SORROW AND MY BEREAVEMENT GO TO WASTE. GATHER UP THE FRAGMENTS, AND AS THE DROP OF WATER IS

ABSORBED BY THE WINE AT THE OFFERTORY OF THE MASS, LET MY LIFE BE ABSORBED IN THINE; LET MY LITTLE CROSS BE ENTWINED WITH THY GREAT CROSS SO THAT I MAY PURCHASE THE JOYS OF EVERLASTING HAPPINESS IN UNION WITH THEE.

"CONSECRATE THESE TRIALS OF MY LIFE WHICH WOULD GO UNREWARDED UNLESS UNITED WITH THEE; TRANSUBSTANTIATE ME SO THAT LIKE BREAD WHICH IS NOW THY BODY, AND WINE WHICH IS NOW THY BLOOD, I TOO MAY BE WHOLLY THINE. I CARE NOT IF THE SPECIES REMAIN, OR THAT, LIKE THE BREAD AND THE WINE I SEEM TO ALL EARTHLY EYES THE SAME AS BEFORE. MY STATION IN LIFE, MY ROUTINE DUTIES, MY WORK, MY FAMILY – ALL THESE ARE BUT THE SPECIES OF MY LIFE WHICH MAY REMAIN UNCHANGED; BUT THE *substance* OF MY LIFE, MY SOUL, MY MIND, MY WILL, MY HEART – TRANSUBSTANTIATE THEM, TRANSFORM THEM WHOLLY INTO THY SERVICE, SO THAT THROUGH ME ALL MAY KNOW HOW SWEET IS THE LOVE OF CHRIST." AMEN.

# THE COMMUNION

*"I thirst."*

OUR BLESSED LORD reaches the communion of His Mass when out from the depths of the Sacred Heart, there wells the cry: "I thirst." This was certainly not a thirst for water, for the earth is His and the fullness thereof; it was not a thirst for any of the refreshing draughts of earth, for He calmed the seas with doors when they burst forth in their fury. When they offered Him a drink, He took it not. It was another kind of thirst which tortured Him. He was thirsty for the souls and hearts of men.

The cry was a cry for communion – the last in a long series of shepherding calls in the quest of God for men. The very fact that it was expressed in the most poignant of all human sufferings, namely, thirst, was the measure of its depth and intensity. Men may *hunger* for God, but God *thirsts* for men. He thirsted for man in Creation as He called him to fellowship with divinity in the garden of Paradise; He thirsted for man in Revelation, as He tried to win back man's erring heart by telling the secrets of His love; He thirsted for man in the Incarnation when He became like the one He loved and was found in the form and habit of man.

Now He was thirsting for man in Redemption, for greater love than this no man hath, that he lay down his life for his friends. It was the final appeal for communion before the curtain rang down on the Great Drama of His earthly life. All the myriad loves of parents for children, of spouse for spouse, if compacted into one great love, would have been the smallest fraction of God's love for man in that cry of thirst. It signified at once, not only how much He thirsted for the little ones, for hungry hearts and empty souls, but also how intense was His desire to satisfy our deepest longing.

Really, there should be nothing mysterious in our thirst for God, for does not the heart pant after the fountain, and the sunflower turn to the sun and the rivers run into the sea? But that He should love us, considering our own unworthiness, and how little our love is worth – *that is the mystery!* And yet such is the meaning of God's thirst for communion with us.

He had already expressed it in the parable of the Lost Sheep when He said He was not satisfied with the ninety-nine; only the lost sheep could give Him perfect joy. Now the truth was expressed again from the Cross: Nothing could adequately satisfy His thirst, but the heart of every man, woman, and child, who were made for Him, and therefore could never be happy until they found their rest in Him.

The basis of this plea for communion is Love, for Love by its very nature tends to unity. Love of citizens one for another begets the unity of the state. Love of man and woman begets the unity of two in one flesh. The love of God for man, therefore, calls for a unity based upon the Incarnation, namely, the unity of all men in the Body and Blood of Christ.

In order, therefore, that God might seal His love for us, He gave us to Himself in Holy Communion, so that as He and His human nature taken from the womb of the Blessed Mother were one in the unity of His Person, so He and we taken from the womb of humanity might be one in the unity of the Mystical Body of Christ. Hence, we use the word "receive" when speaking of communion with our Lord in the Eucharist, for literally we do "receive" Divine Life, just as really and truly as a babe receives the life of its mother.

All life is sustained by communion with a higher life. If the plants could speak, they would say to the moisture and sunlight, "Unless you enter into communion with me, become possessed of my higher laws and powers, you shall not have life in you."

If the animals could speak, they would say to the plants: "Unless you enter into communion with me, you shall not have my higher life in you." We say to all lower creation: "Unless you enter into communion with me, you shall not share in my human life."

Why then should not our Lord say to us: "Unless you enter into communion with Me, you shall not have life in you"? The lower is transformed into, the higher, plants into animals, animals into man, and man, in a more exalted way, becomes "divinized," (if I may use that expression) through and through by the life of Christ.

Communion then is first of all the receiving of Divine Life, a life to which we are no more entitled than marble is entitled to blooming. It is a pure gift of an all-merciful God who so loved us that He willed to be united with us, not in the bonds of flesh, but in the ineffable bonds of the Spirit where love knows no satiety, but only rapture and joy.

And oh, how quickly we should have forgotten Him could we not, like Bethlehem and Nazareth, receive Him into our souls!

Neither gifts nor portraits take the place of the beloved one. And our Lord knew it well. We needed Him, and so He gave us Himself.

But there is another aspect of Communion of which we but rarely think. Communion implies not only *receiving* Divine Life; it means also God *giving* human life. All love is reciprocal. There is no one-sided love, for love by its nature demands mutuality. God thirsts for us, but that means that man must also thirst for God. But do we ever think of Christ receiving Communion from us? Every time we go to the Communion rail, we say we 'receive' Communion, and that is all many of us do, just 'receive Communion.'

There is another aspect of Communion than receiving Divine Life, of which St. John speaks. St. Paul gives us the complementary truth in his Epistle to the Corinthians. Communion is not only an incorporation to the *life* of Christ; it is also an incorporation to His *death*. "As often as you shall eat this bread, and drink the chalice, you shall show the death of the Lord, until He come." (1 Cor. 11:26)

Natural life has two sides: the anabolic and the katabolic. The supernatural also has two sides: the building up of the Christ-pattern and the tearing down of the old Adam. Communion, therefore, implies not only a "receiving" but also a "giving." There can be no ascent to a higher life without death to a lower one. Does not an Easter Sunday presuppose a Good Friday? Does not all love imply mutual self-giving which ends in self-recovery? This being so, should not the Communion rail be a place of exchange, instead of a place of exclusive receiving? Is all the *Life* to pass from Christ to us and nothing to go back in return? Are we to drain the chalice and contribute nothing to its filling? Are we to receive the bread without giving wheat to be ground, to receive the wine and give no grapes to be crushed? If all we did during our lives was to go to Communion to receive Divine Life, to take it away, and leave nothing behind, we would be parasites on the Mystical Body of Christ.

The Pauline injunction bids us fill up in our body the sufferings wanting to the Passion of Christ. We must, therefore, bring a spirit of sacrifice to the Eucharistic table; we must bring the mortification of our lower self, the crosses patiently borne, the crucifixion of our egotism, the death of our concupiscence, and even the very difficulty of our coming to Communion. Then does Communion become what it was always intended to be, namely, a commerce between Christ and the soul, in which we give His Death shown forth in our lives, and He gives

His Life shown forth in our adopted sonship? We give Him our time; He gives us His eternity. We give Him our humanity; He gives us His divinity. We give Him our nothingness; He gives us His all.

Do we really understand the nature of love? Have we not sometimes, in great moments of affection for a little child, said in language which might vary from this, but which expresses the idea, "I love that child so much, I should just like to possess it within myself?" Why? Because all love craves for unity. In the natural order, God has given great pleasures to the unity of the flesh. But those are nothing compared to the pleasure of the unity of the spirit when divinity passes out to humanity, and humanity to divinity – when our will goes to Him, and He comes to us so that we cease to be men and begin to be children of God.

If there has ever been a moment in your life when a fine, noble affection made you feel as if you had been lifted into the third or the seventh heaven; if there has ever been a time in your life when a noble love of a fine human heart cast you into an ecstasy; if there has ever been a time when you have really loved a human heart – then, I ask you, think of what it must be to be united with the great Heart of Love! If the human heart in all of its fine, noble,

Christian riches can so thrill, can so exalt, can make us so ecstatic, then what must be the great heart of Christ? Oh, if the spark is so bright, what must be the flame!

Do we fully realize how much Communion is bound up with Sacrifice, both on the part of our Lord and on the part of us, His poor weak creatures? The Mass makes the two inseparable: there is no Communion without a Consecration. There is no receiving the bread and wine we offer until they have been transubstantiated into the Body and Blood of Christ. Communion is the consequence of the Calvary: namely, we live by what we slay. All nature witnesses this truth; our bodies live by the slaying of the beasts of the fields and the plants of the gardens. We draw life from their crucifixion. We slay them not to destroy, but to fulfill; we immolate them for the sake of communion.

And now by a beautiful paradox of Divine Love, God makes His Cross the very means of our salvation. We have slain Him; we nailed Him there; we crucified Him, but Love in His eternal Heart willed not to be defeated. He willed to give us the very life we slew; to give us the very Food we destroyed; to nourish us with the very Bread we buried, and the very Blood we poured forth. He made our very crime a *happy fault*; He turned a Crucifixion into a Redemption; a Consecration into a Communion; a death into life everlasting.

And it is just that which makes man all the more mysterious! Why man should be loved is no mystery, but why he does not love in return is the great mystery. Why should our Lord be the Great Unloved; why should Love not be loved? Why then, whenever He says: "I thirst," do we give Him vinegar and gall?

# THE ITE, MISSA EST

*"It is finished."*

OUR BLESSED SAVIOUR now comes to the *Ite, missa est* of His Mass, as He utters the cry of triumph: "It is finished."

The work of salvation is finished, but when did it begin? It began back in the agelessness of eternity when God willed to make man. Ever since the beginning of the world, there was a Divine "Impatience" to restore man to the arms of God.

The Word was impatient in heaven to be the 'Lamb slain from the beginning of the world.' He was impatient in prophetic types and symbols, as His dying face was reflected in a hundred mirrors stretching through all Old Testament history. He was impatient to be the real Isaac carrying the wood of His sacrifice in obedience to the commands of His heavenly Abraham. He was impatient to fulfill the mystic symbol of the Lamb of the Jewish Pasch, who was slain without a single bone of its body being broken. He was impatient to be the new Abel, slain by his jealous brethren of the race of Cain that His Blood might cry to Heaven for forgiveness. He was impatient in His mother's womb, as He saluted His precursor John. He was impatient in the Circumcision, as He anticipated His blood-shedding and received the name of "Saviour." He was impatient at the age of twelve, as He reminded His Mother that He had to be about His Father's business. He was impatient in His public life, as He said He had a baptism wherewith He was to be baptized, and He was "straightened until it be accomplished." He was impatient in the Garden, as He turned His back to the consoling twelve legions of angels, to crimson olive roots with His redemptive Blood. He was impatient at His Last Supper, as He anticipated the separation of His Body and Blood under the appearance of bread and wine. And then, impatience closed as the hour of darkness drew near at the end of that Last Supper – He sang. It was the only time He ever sang, the moment He went to His death.

It was a trivial matter for the world if the stars burned brightly, or the mountains stood as symbols of perplexity, or the hills made their tribute to valleys, which gave them birth. What was important was that every single word predicted of Him should be true. Heaven and earth would not pass away until every jot and tittle had been fulfilled. There was only a little iota remaining, one tiny little jot; it was a word of David's about every prediction being fulfilled. Now that all else was fulfilled, He fulfilled that iota; He, the true David, quoted the prophetic David: "It is finished."

*What* is finished? The Redemption of man is finished. Love had completed its mission, for Love had done all that it could. There are two things Love can do. Love by its very nature tends to an Incarnation, and every Incarnation tends to a Crucifixion. Does not all true love tend toward an Incarnation? In the order of human love, does not the affection of husband for wife create from their mutual loves, the incarnation of their confluent love in the form of a child? Once they have begotten their child, do not they make sacrifices for it, even to the point of death? And thus their love tends to a crucifixion.

But this is just a reflection of the divine order, where the love of God for man was so deep and intense that it ended in an Incarnation, which found God in the form and habit of man, whom He loved. But our Lord's love for man did not stop with the Incarnation. Unlike everyone else who was ever born, our Lord came into this world to redeem it. Death was the supreme goal He was seeking. Death interrupted the careers of great men, but it was no interruption to our Lord; it was His crowning glory; it was the unique goal He was seeking.

His Incarnation thus tended to the Crucifixion, for "greater love than this no man has, that he lay down his life for his friends" (John 15:13). Now that Love had run its course in the Redemption of man, Divine Love could say: "I have done all for my vineyard that I can do." Love can do no more than die. It is finished: "Ite, missa est."

*His* work is finished. But is ours? When He said, "it is finished," He did not mean that the opportunities of His life had ended; He meant that His work was done so perfectly that nothing could be added to it to make it more perfect – but with us, how seldom that is true. Too many of us end our lives, but few of us see them *finished*. A sinful life may end, but a sinful life is never a finished life.

If our lives just "end," our friends will ask: "How much did he leave?" But if our life is "finished" our friends will ask: "How much did he take with him?" A finished life is not measured by years but by deeds; not by the time spent in the vineyard, but by the work done. In a short time, a man may fulfill many years; even those who come at the eleventh hour may finish their lives; even those who come to God like the thief at the last breath may finish their lives in the Kingdom of God. Not for them the sad word of regret: "Too late, O ancient Beauty, have I loved Thee."

Our Lord finished His work, but we have not finished ours. He pointed the way we must follow. He laid down the Cross at the finish, but we must take it up. He finished Redemption in His physical Body, but we have not finished it in His Mystical Body. He has finished salvation; we have not yet applied it to our souls. He has finished the Temple, but we must live in it. He has finished the model Cross; we must fashion ours to its pattern. He has finished sowing the seed; we must reap the harvest. He has finished filling the chalice, but we have not finished drinking its refreshing draughts. He has planted the wheat field; we must gather it into our barns. He has finished the Sacrifice of Calvary; we must finish the Mass.

The Crucifixion was not meant to be an inspirational drama, but a pattern act on which to model our lives. We are not meant to sit and watch the Cross as something done and ended like the life of Socrates. *What was done on Calvary avails for us only in the degree that we repeat it in our own lives.*

The Mass makes this possible, for at the renewal of Calvary on our altars we are not on-lookers but sharers in Redemption, and there it is that we "finish" our work. He has told us: "And I if I be lifted up from the earth, will draw all things to myself" (John 12:32). He finished His work when He was lifted up on the Cross; we finish ours when we permit Him to draw us unto Himself in the Mass.

The Mass is that which makes the cross visible to every eye; it placards the Cross at all the crossroads of civilization; it brings Calvary so close that even tired feet can make the journey to its sweet embrace; every hand may now reach out to touch its Sacred Burden, and every ear may hear its sweet appeal, for the Mass and the Cross, are the same. In both there is the same offering of a perfectly surrendered will of the beloved Son, the same Body broken, the same Blood flowed forth, the same Divine Forgiveness. All that has been said and done and acted during Holy Mass is to be taken away with us, lived, practiced, and woven into all the circumstances and conditions of our daily lives. His sacrifice is made our sacrifice by making it the oblation of ourselves in union with Him; His life given for us becomes our life given for Him. Thus do we return from Mass as those who have made their choice, turned their backs upon the world, and become other Christs for the generation in which we live – living potent witnesses to the Love that died that we might live with Love.

This world of ours is full of half-completed Gothic cathedrals, of half-finished lives and half-crucified souls. Some carry the Cross to Calvary and then abandon it; others are nailed to it and detach themselves before the elevation; others are crucified, but in answer to the challenge of the world "Come down," they come down after one hour . . . two hours . . . after two hours and fifty-nine minutes. Real Christians are they who persevere unto the end. Our Lord stayed until He had finished.

The priest must likewise stay at the altar until the Mass is finished. He may not come down. So we must stay with the Cross until our lives are finished. Christ on the Cross is the pattern and model of a finished life. Our human nature is the raw material; our will is the chisel; God's grace is the energy and the inspiration.

Touching the chisel to our unfinished nature, we first cut off huge chunks of selfishness. Then by more delicate chiselings, we dig away smaller bits of egotism until finally only a brush of the hand is needed to bring out the completed masterpiece – a finished man made to the image and likeness of the pattern on the Cross. We are at the altar under the symbol of bread and wine; we have offered ourselves to our Lord; He has consecrated us.

We must therefore not take ourselves back, but remain there unto the end, praying unceasingly, that when the lease of our life has ended, and we look back upon a life lived in intimacy with the Cross, the echo of the Sixth Word may ring out on our lips: "It is finished."

And as the sweet accents of that Ite, missa est reach beyond the corridors of Time and pierce the "hid battlements of eternity," the angel choirs and the white-robed army of the Church Triumphant will answer back: "*Deo Gratias.*"

# THE LAST GOSPEL

*"Father, into thy hands,*

*I commend my spirit."*

IT IS A BEAUTIFUL paradox that the Last Gospel of the Mass takes us back to the beginning, for it opens with the words "In the beginning." And such is life: the last of this life is the beginning of the next. Fittingly indeed, then, that the Last Word of our Lord was His Last Gospel: "Father, into thy hands, I commend my spirit." Like the Last Gospel of the Mass, it too takes Him back to the beginning, for He now goes back to the Father whence He came. He has completed His work. He began His Mass with the word: "Father." And He ends it with the same word.

"Everything perfect," the Greeks would say, "travels in circles." Just as the great planets only after a long period of time complete their orbits, and then go back again to their starting point, as if to salute Him who sent them on their way, so the Word Incarnate, who came down to say His Mass, now completes His earthly career and goes back again to His heavenly Father who sent Him on the journey of the world's redemption. The Prodigal Son is about to return to His Father's House, for is He not the Prodigal Son? Thirty-three years ago He left the Father's House and the blessedness of heaven and came down to this earth of ours, which is a foreign country – for every country is foreign which is away from the Father's House.

For thirty-three years, He had been spending His substance. He spent the substance of His Truth in the infallibility of His Church; He spent the substance of His Power in the authority He gave to His apostles and their successors. He spent the substance of His Life in the Redemption and the Sacraments. Now every drop of it is gone, He looks longingly back again to the Father's House, and with a loud cry throws His Spirit into His Father's arms, not in the attitude of one who is taking a plunge into the darkness, but as one who knows where He is going – to a homecoming with His Father.

In that Last Word and Last Gospel, which took Him back to the Beginning of all beginnings, namely, His Father is revealed the history and rhythm of life. The end of all things must, in some way, get back to their beginning. As the Son goes back to the Father; as Nicodemus must be born again; as the body returns to the dust – so the soul of man, which came from God, must one day go back to God.

Death is not the end of all. The cold clod falling upon the grave does not mark finis to the history of a man. The way he has lived in this life determines how he shall live in the next. If he has sought God during life, death will be like the opening of a cage, enabling him to use his wings to fly to the arms of the divine Beloved. If he has fled from God during life, death will be the beginning of an eternal flight away from Life and Truth and Love – and that is hell.

Before the throne of God, whence we came on our earthly novitiate, we must one day go back to render an account of our stewardship. There will not be a human creature who, when the last sheaf is garnered, will not be found either to have accepted or rejected the divine gift of Redemption and in accepting or rejecting it to have signed the warrant of his eternal destiny.

As the sales on a cash register are recorded for the end of our business day, so our thoughts, words, and deeds are recorded for the final Judgment. If we but live in the shadow of the Cross, death will not be an ending but a beginning of eternal life. Instead of a parting, it will be a meeting; instead of a going away, it will be an arriving; instead of being an end, it will be a Last Gospel – a return to the beginning. As a voice whispers, "You must leave the earth," the Father's voice will say, "My child, come unto Me."

We have been sent into this world as children of God, to assist at the Holy Sacrifice of the Mass. We are to take our stand at the foot of the Cross and, like those who stood under it the first day, we will be asked to declare our loyalties. God has given us the wheat and the grapes of life, and as the men who, in the Gospel, were given talents; we will have to show return on that divine gift.

God has given us our lives as wheat and grapes. It is our duty to consecrate them and bring them back to God as bread and wine – transubstantiated, divinized, and spiritualized. There must be harvest in our hands after the springtime of the earthly pilgrimage.

That is why Calvary is erected in the midst of us, and we are on its sacred hill. We were not made to be mere on-lookers, shaking our dice like the executioners of old, but rather to be participants in the mystery of the Cross.

If there is any way to picture Judgment in terms of the Mass, it is to picture it in the way the Father greeted His Son, namely, by looking at His hands. They bore the marks of labour, the callouses of redemption, and the scars of salvation. So too, when our earthly pilgrimage is over, and we go back to the beginning, God will look at both of our hands. If our hands in life touched the hands of His divine Son they will bear the same livid marks of nails; if our feet in life have trod over the same road that leads to eternal glory through the detour of a rocky and thorny Calvary, they too shall bear the same bruises; if our hearts beat in unison with His, then they too shall show the riven side which the wicked lance of jealous earth did pierce.

Blessed indeed are they who carry in their Cross-marked hands the bread and wine of consecrated lives signed with the sign and sealed with the seal of redemptive Love. But woe unto them who come from Calvary with hands unscarred and white.

God grant that when life is over, and the earth is vanishing like a dream of one awakening when eternity is flooding our souls with its splendours, we may with humble and triumphant faith re-echo the Last Word of Christ: "Father, into thy hands I commend my spirit."

And so the Mass of Christ ends. The *Confiteor* was His prayer to the Father for the forgiveness of our sins; the *Offertory* was the presentation on the paten of the Cross of small hosts of the thief and ourselves; the *Sanctus* was His commending ourselves to Mary, the Queen of Saints; the *Consecration* was the separation of His Blood from His Body, and the seeming separation of divinity and humanity; the *Communion* was His thirst for the souls of men; the *Ite, missa est* was the finishing of the work of salvation; the *Last Gospel* was the return to the Father whence He came.

And now that the Mass is over, and He has commended His Spirit to the Father, He prepares to give back His Body to His Blessed Mother at the foot of the Cross. Thus once again will the end be the beginning, for at the beginning of His earthly life He was nestled on her lap in Bethlehem, and now, on Calvary, He will take His place there once again.

Earth had been cruel to Him; His feet wandered after lost sheep, and we dug them with steel; His hands stretched out the Bread of everlasting life, and we fastened them with nails; His lips spoke the Truth, and we sealed them with dust. He came to give us Life, and we took away His. But that was our fatal mistake. We really did not take it away. We only tried to take it away. He laid it down of Himself. Nowhere do the Evangelists say that He died. They say, "He gave up the spirit." It was a willing, self-determined relinquishment of life.

It was not death which approached Him; it was He who approached death. That is why, as the end draws near, the Saviour commands the portal of death to open unto Him in the presence of the Father. The chalice is gradually being drained of its rich red wine of salvation. The rocks of earth open their hungry mouths to drink as if more thirsty for the draughts of salvation than the parched hearts of man; the earth itself shook in horror because men had erected God's Cross upon its breast. Magdalene, the penitent, as usual, clings to His feet, and there she will be again Easter morn; John, the priest, with a face like a cast moulded out of love, listens to the beating of the Heart whose secrets He learned and loved and mastered; Mary thinks how different Calvary is from Bethlehem.

Thirty-three years ago, Mary looked down at His sacred face; now He looks down at her. In Bethlehem, heaven looked up into the face of earth; now, the roles are reversed. Earth looks up into the face of heaven – but a heaven marred by the scars of earth. He loved her above all the creatures of earth, for she was His Mother and the Mother of us all. He saw her first on coming to earth; He shall see her last on leaving it. Their eyes meet, all aglow with life, speaking a language all their own. There is a rupture of a heart through a rapture of love, then a bowed head, a broken heart. Back to the hands of God, He gives, pure and sinless, His spirit, in loud and ringing voice that trumpets eternal victory. And Mary stands alone a Childless Mother. Jesus is dead!

Mary looks up into His eyes which are so clear even in the face of death: "High Priest of Heaven and earth, Thy Mass is finished! Leave the altar of the Cross and repair into Thy Sacristy. As High Priest Thou didst come forth from the sacristy of Heaven, panoplied in the vestments of humanity and bearing Thy Body as Bread and Thy Blood as Wine.

Now the Sacrifice has been consummated. The Consecration bell has rung. Thou didst offer Thy Spirit to Thy Father; Thy Body and Thy Blood to man. There remains now nothing but the drained chalice. Enter into Thy Sacristy. Take off the garments of mortality and put on the white robes of immortality. Show Thy hands, and feet, and side to Thy heavenly Father and say: "With these was I wounded in the house of those that love me."

"Enter, High Priest, into Thy heavenly Sacristy, and as Thy earthly ambassadors hold aloft the Bread and Wine, do Thou show Thyself to the Father in loving intercession for us even unto the consummation of the world. Earth has been cruel to Thee, but Thou wilt be kind to earth. Earth lifted Thee on the Cross, but now Thou shalt lift earth unto the Cross. Open the door of the heavenly Sacristy, O High Priest! Behold, it is now we who stand at the door and knock!

"And Mary, what shall we say to Thee? Mary, Thou art the Sacristan of the High Priest! Thou wert a Sacristan in Bethlehem when He did come to Thee as wheat and grapes in the crib of Bethlehem. Thou wert His Sacristan at the Cross, where He became the Living Bread and Wine through the Crucifixion. Thou art His Sacristan now, as He comes from the altar of the Cross wearing only the drained chalice of His sacred Body.

"As that chalice is laid in your lap it may seem that Bethlehem has come back again, for He is once more yours. But it only seems – for in Bethlehem He was the chalice whose gold was to be tried by fire, but now at Calvary, He is the chalice whose gold has passed through the fires of Golgotha and Calvary. In Bethlehem He was white as He came from the Father: now He is red as He came from us. But thou art still His Sacristan! And as the Immaculate Mother of all hosts who go to the altar, do thou, O Virgin Mary, send us there pure, and keep us pure, even unto the day when we enter into the heavenly Sacristy of the Kingdom of Heaven, where thou wilt be our eternal Sacristan and He our eternal Priest."

And you, friends of the Crucified, your High Priest has left the Cross, but He has left us the Altar. On the Cross He was alone; in the Mass, He is with us. On the Cross He suffered in His physical Body; on the altar, He suffers in the Mystical Body which we are. On the Cross He was the unique Host; in the Mass, we are the small hosts, and He the large host receiving His Calvary through us. On the Cross He was the wine; in the Mass, we are the drop of water united with the wine and consecrated with Him. In that sense He is still on the Cross, still saying the Confiteor with us, still forgiving us, still commending us to Mary, still thirsting for us, still drawing us unto the Father, for as long as sin remains on earth, still will the Cross remain.


"Whenever there is silence around me
By day or by night –
I am startled by a cry.
It came down from the Cross.

The first time I heard it
I went out and searched –
And found a man in the throes of Crucifixion.

And I said: 'I will take you down,'
and I tried to take the nails out of His Feet,
But He said: 'Let them be for I cannot be taken
down until every man, every woman, and every
child come together to take me down.'

And I said: 'But I cannot bear your cry. What
can I do?'
And He said: 'Go about the world –
Tell everyone that you meet –
There is a Man on the Cross.'"

*Elizabeth Cheney*

# ACKNOWLEDGMENTS

To the members of the Archbishop Fulton John Sheen Foundation in Peoria, Illinois. In particular, to the Most Rev. Daniel R. Jenky, C.S.C., Bishop of Peoria, for your leadership and fidelity to the cause of Sheen's canonization and the creation of this book.

www.archbishopsheencause.org

To the staff at Sophia Institute Press for their invaluable assistance in sharing the writings of Archbishop Fulton J. Sheen to a new generation of readers.

www.sophiainstitute.com

To the volunteers at the Archbishop Fulton J. Sheen Mission Society of Canada: your motto "Unless Souls are Saved, Nothing is Saved", speaks to the reality that Jesus Christ came into the world to make salvation available to all souls.

www.archbishopfultonjsheenmissionsocietyofcanada.org

To the good folks at 'Bishop Sheen Today'. We value your guidance, support, and prayers in helping us to share the wisdom of Archbishop Fulton J. Sheen. Your apostolic work of sharing his audio and video presentations along with his many writings to a worldwide audience is very much appreciated.

www.bishopsheentoday.com

And lastly, to Archbishop Fulton J. Sheen, whose teachings on Our Lord's Passion and His Seven Last Words continue to inspire me to love God more and to appreciate the gift of the Church. May we be so blessed as to imitate Archbishop Sheen's love for the saints, the sacraments, the Eucharist, and the Blessed Virgin Mary. May the Good Lord grant him a very high place in heaven!

# ABOUT THE AUTHOR

## Fulton J. Sheen
## *(1895–1979)*

Archbishop Sheen, best known for his popularly televised and syndicated television program, Life is Worth Living, is held today as one of Catholicism's most widely recognized figures of the twentieth century.

Fulton John Sheen, born May 8, 1895, in El Paso, Illinois was raised and educated in the Roman Catholic faith. Originally named Peter John Sheen, he came to be known as a young boy by his mother's maiden name, Fulton. He was ordained a priest of the Diocese of Peoria at St. Mary's Cathedral in Peoria, IL on September 20, 1919.

Following his ordination, Sheen studied at the Catholic University of Louvain, where he earned a doctorate in philosophy in 1923. That same year, he received the Cardinal Mercier Prize for International Philosophy, becoming the first-ever American to earn this distinction.

Upon returning to America, after varied and extensive work throughout Europe, Sheen continued to preach and teach theology and philosophy from 1927 to 1950, at the Catholic University of America in Washington DC.

Beginning in 1930, Sheen hosted a weekly Sunday night radio broadcast called 'The Catholic Hour'. This broadcast captured many devoted listeners, reportedly drawing an audience of four million people every week for over twenty years.

In 1950, he became the National Director of the Society for the Propagation of the Faith, raising funds to support missionaries. During the sixteen years that he held this position, millions of dollars were raised to support the missionary activity of the Church. These efforts influenced tens of millions of people all over the world, bringing them to know Christ and his Church. In addition, his preaching and personal example brought about many converts to Catholicism.

In 1951, Sheen was appointed Auxiliary Bishop of the Archdiocese of New York. That same year, he began hosting his television program 'Life is Worth Living', which lasted for six years.

In the course of its run, that program competed for airtime with popular television programs hosted by the likes of Frank Sinatra and Milton Berle. Sheen's program held its own, and in 1953, just two years after its debut, he won an Emmy Award for "Most Outstanding Television Personality." Fulton Sheen credited the Gospel writers - Matthew, Mark, Luke, and John - for their valuable contribution to his success. Sheen's television show ran until 1957, boasting as many as thirty million weekly viewers.

In the Fall of 1966, Sheen was appointed Bishop of Rochester, New York. During that time, Bishop Sheen hosted another television series, 'The Fulton Sheen Program' which ran from 1961 to 1968, closely modeling the format of his 'Life is Worth Living' series.

After nearly three years as Bishop of Rochester, Fulton Sheen resigned and was soon appointed by Pope Paul VI as Titular Archbishop of the See of Newport, Wales. This new appointment allowed Sheen the flexibility to continue preaching.

Another claim to fame was Bishop Sheen's annual Good Friday homilies, which he preached for fifty-eight consecutive years at St. Patrick's Cathedral in New York City, and elsewhere. Sheen also led numerous retreats for priests and religious, preaching at conferences all over the world.

When asked by Pope St. Pius XII how many converts he had made, Sheen responded, "Your Holiness, I have never counted them. I am always afraid that if I did count them, I might think I made them, instead of the Lord."

Sheen was known for being approachable and down to earth. He used to say, "If you want people to stay as they are, tell them what they want to hear. If you want to improve them, tell them what they should know." This he did, not only in his preaching but also through his numerous books and articles. His book titled 'Peace of Soul' was sixth on the New York Times best-seller list.

Three of Sheen's great loves were: the missions and the propagation of the faith; the Holy Mother of God and the Eucharist.

He made a daily holy hour of prayer before the Blessed Sacrament. It was from Jesus Himself that he drew strength and inspiration to preach the gospel, and in the Presence of Whom that he prepared his homilies. "I beg [Christ] every day to keep me strong physically and alert mentally, in order to preach His gospel and proclaim His Cross and Resurrection," he said. "I am so happy doing this that I sometimes feel that when I come to the good Lord in Heaven, I will take a few days' rest and then ask Him to allow me to come back again to this earth to do some more work."

His contributions to the Catholic Church are numerous and varied, ranging from educating in classrooms, churches, and homes, to preaching over a nationally publicized radio show, and two television programs, as well as penning over sixty written works. Archbishop Fulton J. Sheen had a gift for communicating the Word of God in the most pure, simple way. His strong background in philosophy helped him to relate to everyone in a highly personalized manner. His timeless messages continue to have great relevance today. His goal was to inspire everyone to live a God-centered life with the joy and love that God intended.

On October 2, 1979, Archbishop Sheen received his greatest accolade, when Pope St. John Paul II embraced him at St. Patrick's Cathedral in New York City. The Holy Father said to him, "You have written and spoken well of the Lord Jesus. You are a loyal son of the Church."

The good Lord called Fulton Sheen home on December 9, 1979. His television broadcasts now available through various media, and his books, extend his earthly work of winning souls for Christ. Sheen's cause for canonization was opened in 2002. In 2012, Pope Benedict XVI declared him 'Venerable', and in July of 2019, Pope Francis formally approved the miracle necessary for Sheen's beatification and canonization process to move forward. The time and date for the church to declare Archbishop Fulton J. Sheen a saint is in God's hands.

J.M.J.

## Books Available Through
## Bishop Sheen Today Publishing

The Rainbow of Sorrow

The Seven Last Words

Calvary and the Mass

Love One Another

The Cross and the Beatitudes

The Cross and the Crisis

Love One Another

Victory Over Vice

The Seven Virtues

For God and Country

God and War

The Divine Verdict

God Love You

The Seven Last Words Explained

The Priest Is Not His Own

The Cross and the Crib

Philosophies at War

The Seven Last Words of Christ Explained

Father, Forgive Them for They Know Not What They Do.

This Day Thou Shall Be with Me in Paradise

Woman Behold Your Son; Behold Your Mother

My God! My God! Why Hast Thou Forsaken Me?

I Thirst

It is Finished

Father Into Your Hands I Commend My Spirit

Liberty, Equality and Fraternity

Missions and the World Crisis

Seven Words to the Cross

Seven Pillars of Peace

The Holy Hour Prayer Book

Seven Words of Jesus & Mary

*www.bishopsheentoday.com*